A Most Heavenly Children's Christmas Musical

Created by Don & Lorie Marsh

PUBLISHING COMPANY

Kansas City, MO 64141

CONTENTS

Characters (in order of appearance)

MOON   Female Adult, Teen or mature Child;
a warm, patient and yet overly dramatic at times

VEGA   Boy; a street smart kid with a good heart

POLARIS   Boy; surfer dude type, fun loving

QUASAR   Girl; sweet innocent little star

ZENITH   Girl; diva hollywood type

PULSAR   Boy; from the Caribbean

(Moon is on an empty stage, dressed in black with a crescent moon shape on a shirt that is lit up with a black light. Music begins)

MOON *(very dramatic)*: Before there was light, before there was anything we know or understand today, HE was...and He is LIGHT! Pure, flawless, brilliant, incandescent, resplendent light! And at the time of His choosing He flung His hand across the sky, spoke the word, and we came to be!

Since that time we have been on a journey under the direction of Jesus the Morning Star. Our job? To illustrate the beauty of the Father...to illuminate the truth of the glory of God and His illustrious Son. Our mission? To boldly go where no star has gone before...Earth, the final frontier!

Star Journey Opener

Words and Music by
DON and LORIE MARSH
Arranged by Don Marsh

* Music by Richard Strauss. Arr. © 2000 by Pilot Point Music(ASCAP). All rights reserved. Administered by The Copyright Company, 40 Music Square East, Nashville, TN 37203.

bright, On the star

jour - ney far. Un - der - neath our star - lit

sky, Christ the Sav - ior comes to lie.

We will shine On His birth!

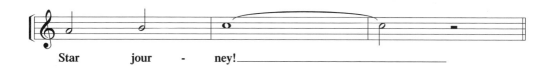

Star jour - ney!

Ev - er - read - y to re - veal the glo - ry of His

birth, And to help you cel - e - brate the

6

day He came_____ to earth!_____

We are shin-ing thro' the night, From a con-stel - la - tion

bright, On the__ star_____

jour - ney__ far._____ Come with us a - long our

way, Trav - 'ling on to Christ-mas day.

We will__ shine_____ on His__ birth!_____

Star jour - ney!_____

VEGA: That was cosmic Moon! Totally cosmic! *(to audience)* Moon here was just filling you guys in on us stars. She likes to wax eloquent about things like this, especially our creation. Sometimes she goes through a phase where she wanes a little about everything. You know, month in, month out...waxing and waning...waxing and waning. But, hey man, you just gotta love that ol' Moon, she's like, a little orbital! *(twirls finger around)*

MOON: Well, it is the most amazing story...the story of our creation. Of course, it's completely eclipsed in light of how God sent His own Son to the earthlings. Now that's the most astronomical story I've ever heard!

VEGA: Yeah man, it is far and above the tale that blasts us out of the sky. Every year we stars and starlets "cluster together" and throw a far-out bash we call a "Constellation party." You'll have to, like, scope it out sometime.

MOON: Here, from our observatory we share our star stories. Each star reflects on his observations as he's watched the earth make its journey around the sun. But, every year the story of the first Christmas seems to be the hands down favorite, by light years! Of course, I always so enjoy the one some of those silly earthlings came up with about how the universe was created.

VEGA *(laughing)*: Oh, yeah, I always get a "big bang" out of that one!

(MOON laughs)

VEGA: Hey! The light just went on! Now here's an idea for ya'. What do you think, Moon-maid? Should we, like, crash the "Constellation party" with these here earthlings?

MOON: Affirmative, Vega, what a brilliant idea! *(claps and turns to audience)* Oh, please, dear earthlings, won't you give us the honor of joining us on our star journey? Come to our party here in our starlight observatory and see the Christmas story with *(laughing, pretending to hold binoculars up to her eyes dramatically)* stars in your eyes.

VEGA: There you go again, Moon girl, making me laugh! But don't get me off course here, let's get this party rockin'. *(He sees Polaris coming and calls him into the observatory.)* Hey, Polaris! Come in man. Yo, Polaris!

POLARIS *(enters)*: Greetings, fellow star dudes. Sorry, for taking so long to come into view, I was just getting a little liquid refreshment over at the Milky Way with my friend that sweet little Nova, and,well, I guess I just spaced out.

MOON *(interrupting)*: Polaris, please help us get our "Constellation party" under way. Won't you reveal to us the details of your story?

POLARIS: Hey, your Moonliness, let me tell you, it was a real kick in the comet! Check this out. The other night, you know, about 2000 years ago, I was scoping out this earthling Joseph and, like, he was having this totally cosmic dream! This angel, I think it was Gabriel or something, told him that his true love, Mary, was going to have a little nebula...I mean, a baby! But this kid-to-come was no ordinary earthling. He was the Son of God. The Creator, Himself, in miniature, *(music begins)* spark-size form! Then Joseph woke up. Man, he was all confused too. He came outside to have a little talk with me. I got a few of my friends together to back me up and this is what we said.

His Name Is Jesus

Words and Music by
DON and LORIE MARSH
Arranged by Don Marsh

maz-ing, yet true,_____ that God has cho - sen you, To tell the
maz-ing, yet true,_____ that God has cho - sen you, To tell the

Group 1

world   the name of His Boy._____ And His
world   the name of His Son._____

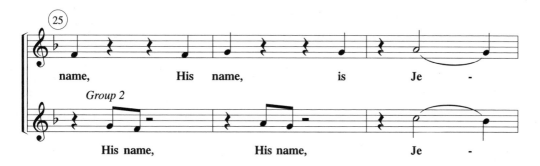

name,   His name,   is   Je -

Group 2

His name,   His name,   Je -

sus._____ God with us,_____ Im - man - u - el;_

sus._____ God with us,_____ Im - man - u - el;_

_____   For He'll   save,   He'll

_____   He'll save,

VEGA: Quasar! Hey, girl! Tell us your story!

(QUASAR joins the group of stars on stage and speaks to audience)

QUASAR: I was in the star observatory that night watching the earth. I saw the earthling, Mary, looking up into my constellation. I tried my best to twinkle and glow and show her the Creator's glory so she would know how great He is. Mary praised the Creator in that special way that only earthlings can. She called Him Lord *(music begins)* and told Him that she would do whatever He asked. It was the most beautiful sight I've ever seen on my star journey!

Star Light, Star Bright

Words and Music by
DON and LORIE MARSH
Arranged by Don Marsh

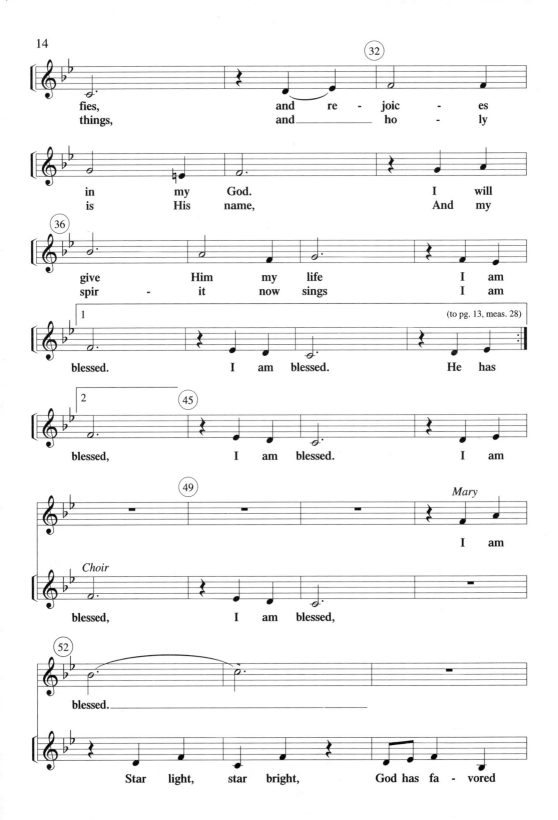

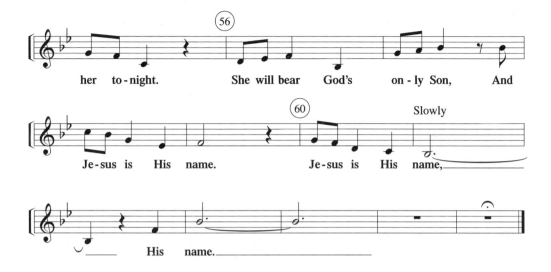

her to-night. She will bear God's on-ly Son, And Je-sus is His name. Je-sus is His name,___ ___ His name.___

(ZENITH rushes onto stage, slightly out of breath and completely full of herself.)

ZENITH: I'm here! I'm here! It's me, the Great Zenith! So sorry to have kept my fans waiting, but a true star must always be fashionably late! *(to audience)* You must hear my story, for it was I *(pauses dramatically and strikes a pompous pose)* whose effervescent hues so brilliantly lit the pathway to Bethlehem for Mary and Joseph! Obviously, *(overly dramatic)* the Creator gave me this extra lovely, luminous quality because He knew I would be the perfect one to help them arrive safely! A truly galactic performance.

MOON *(to audience and VEGA)*: Looks like I'm not the only one who "waxes" around here. *(to ZENITH)* My dear, lest we become too proud of ourselves, need I remind you it was the Creator's plan for the Baby to be born in Bethlehem of Judea. He provided a sky full of stars to light their way. It is He who safely directs the earthling's path when they follow Him. He knows their final destination. *(music begins)*

God Knows Your Destination

Words and Music by
DON and LORIE MARSH
Arranged by Don Marsh

1. At times it might seem real - ly hard, fol - low - ing the Lord. But He'll be right there by your side, help - ing you to know. That God knows, God knows.

2. The words that Mar - y heard that day are the same to - day. The Fa - ther has a plan for you, do not be a - fraid. For God knows, God knows.

God knows your des - ti - na - tion. Fol - low with

no hes - i - ta - tion, He knows what's best_____ for

(to pg. 16, meas. 3)

you. He's prom - ised to see_____ you through.

God sees the big pic - ture, He has a Mas - ter

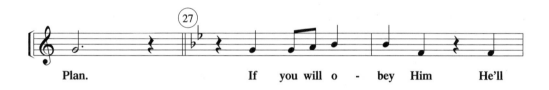

Plan. If you will o - bey Him He'll

help you un - der - stand!_____

God knows,_____ God knows._____ God knows_____your

des - ti - na - tion. Fol - low_____with no hes - i - ta - tion,

He knows what's best ____ for you. He's

prom-ised to see ____ you through.

He knows what's best ____ for you, He's

prom-ised to see ____ you through. ____

(Choir on stage begins to baa and bleat like sheep at random, starting with one voice and building.)

MOON: It was a gloooorious night! I don't know why I especially remember the sheep?

VEGA: That's not a sound you can easily wipe from the ol' memory banks *(stars join the choir in bleating)* Baa...Baa...!

(music begins)

MOON: Oh, but there we were. The scene was set. There were shepherds asleep on the hillside, unaware that the planets, the stars, all of heaven and earth were waiting, watching, ready to split our atoms. When suddenly, throughout the celestial heavens, the sky exploded with ten thousand angels in chorus!

Glory to God in the Highest!

Words and Music by
DON and LORIE MARSH
Arranged by Don Marsh

*Zenith holds top cue note after choir cuts off.

PLEASE NOTE: Copying of this product is not covered by CCLI licenses. For CCLI information call 1-800-234-2446.

(When the choir and stage stars cut off, ZENITH, who has stepped forward taking an operatic pose, continues to hold the note dramatically. After her cut-off she takes a bow, throws her boa over her shoulder, spins and walks off. The choir and stage stars clap softly and politely while stifling their giggles.)

MOON *(rolling her eyes)*: Thank you Zenith for your lovely rendition of the events. *(sarcastic chuckle)* Ahhh, yes, and how well I remember what the angel said that night, "Do not be afraid, for I bring you good tidings of great joy which shall be to all people. Today in the town of David a Savior has been born to you. He is Christ the Lord. This shall be a sign unto you. You shall find the baby, wrapped in cloths, lying in a manger."

ZENITH: Oh, my dears, there's never been a better reason for a party.

VEGA: That night all of heaven and earth got down! *(music begins)*

Heaven and Nature Sing

with
Joy to the World
For Unto Us a Child Is Born
The First Noel

Words and Music by
DON and LORIE MARSH
Arranged by Don Marsh

*"Joy to the World"
Opt: add congregation

Joy to the world! the Lord is come; Let earth re - ceive her King. Let ev - 'ry heart pre - pare Him room, And heav'n and na - ture sing, And heav'n and na - ture sing, And heav'n, and heav'n and na - ture sing.

22

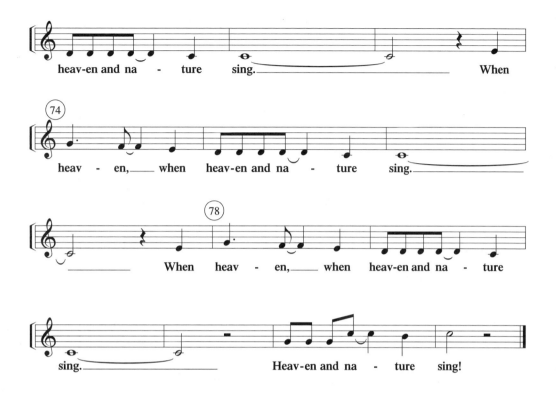

QUASAR *(clasping hands together)*: Oh, my favorite part of the story is coming up. Remember, the shepherds went into Bethlehem and found the precious Baby Jesus?

MOON: Oh yes, and as we bathed the sleepy little town in starlight, Mary brought forth her first born Son and laid Him in a manger. *(music begins)*

O Little Town of Bethlehem

PHILLIPS BROOKS

LEWIS H. REDNER
Arranged by Don Marsh

1. O
2. For

lit - tle town___ of Beth - le - hem,___ How
Christ is born___ of Mar - y;___ And,

still we___ see thee lie! A - bove thy deep___ and
gath - ered___ all a - bove, While mor - tals sleep,___ the

dream - less sleep___ The si - lent___ stars go
an - gels keep___ Their watch of___ won - d'ring

by. Yet in thy dark___ streets shin - eth The
love. O morn - ing stars,___ to - geth - er Pro -

ev - er - last - ing light; The hopes and fears___ of
claim the ho - ly birth; And prais - es sing___ to

PLEASE NOTE: Copying of this product is not covered by CCLI licenses. For CCLI information call 1-800-234-2446.

POLARIS *(reverently)*: Now that is far out! Our Creator, I mean the most holy Lord God, became a tiny baby and was laid in a manger. His love for these earthlings is like totally awesome!

MOON: And isn't it so very curious that the earthlings think light comes from the sun? From up here in our observatory we see things so much more clearly. If only they could see with their hearts, instead of with their telescopes they would know that true light comes not from the sun of the Solar System, but from the Son of God, Jesus, the Bright and Morning Star. *(music begins)*

Morning Star

Words and Music by
DON and LORIE MARSH
Arranged by Don Marsh

heart of mine,____ Emp - ty as____ could be! Then

(45) Je - sus came____ and brought me the light,____

Sud - den - ly I could see. God was - n't just____ in the

sky a - bove____ But He is here____ where we are. And

(53) now I'm His child____ and I live in His love,____

Je - sus, the Bright and Morn - ing Star.

D.S. al Coda (to pg. 27, meas. 23) CODA (61)

O____ Star. Our Bright and

(6) Morn - ing Star.____

(Maracas are heard as PULSAR enters. PULSAR is a Caribbean character and enters excited and clapping hands.)

QUASAR: Here he comes, it's Pulsar, the brightest star of all!

PULSAR: Hallooo everybody. *(dances into center of stage)* Hallo, lovely morning Vega "mon". Pulsar is here for da Christmas party. *(maracas stop)* I have moooved into place to tell you of da wondrous night when I led da Wise Men to da manger of da Christ Child. Oh, such fun we had. *(maracas begin)* Come on twinkle-toes you can do it to! I just know you can!

(PULSAR "cha-chas" over to ZENITH and tries to get her to join a conga line with the other stars)

ZENITH: Not this "twinkle-toes", Buster! *(Maracas stop as she tosses boa over her shoulder and acts condescending.)*

VEGA *(backs away when PULSAR approaches)*: No way, man...my "cha-cha's" in the shop for repair. How come we have to go through this year after year, anyway?

PULSAR: Because my little friend, I just gotta move! It's just da way da Creator made me. Oh, and dat is why I was the one to guide the Wise Men. Quite a journey too. *(music starts)* And all da way from da east to where da little King was. But, oh such things we saw along the way. Such fun, such fun! *(Wise Men join the Conga line and end up at the microphones just in time for the solos.)*

Star of Wonder

with
We Three Kings

Words and Music by
DON and LORIE MARSH
Arranged by Don Marsh

Bright Calypso ♩ = ca. 104

Star of won - der   shine your light___ up - on   us,

Star of won - der   shine your light___ up - on   us,

now.
1. Far   a - way   in a
2. For   so___ long,   near - ly

dis - tant___ land   with their   tel - e - scopes   in their
all   their___ lives   They had   looked   for___ just,   such a

king - ly___ hands.   Peer - ing___ up   in - to   the
love - ly___ sight.   Now   they___ cross,   they're cross - ing

Copyright © 2000 by Pilot Point Music (ASCAP). All rights reserved.
Administered by The Copyright Company, 40 Music Square East, Nashville, TN 37203.

star - ry___ night, Then they saw a vi - sion bright!
sand - y___ seas, Won - d'ring "What could this___ light be?"

1 (to pg. 30, meas. 17) | 2   26 *"We Three Kings"

Star of won - der,___

Star of light,___ Star with roy - al___

beau - ty bright.___ West - ward lead - ing still___

___ pro - ceed - ing, Guide us to___ your per - fect

light!

35
3. And they're___ sure that this grand new___ star, That's been
4. Gold and___ myrrh, Frank - in - cense they___ bring, As a

lead - ing___ them, O so ver - y___ far,
birth - day___ gift for the in - fant__ King,

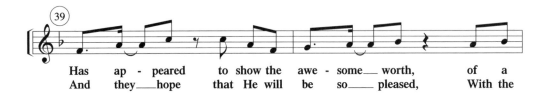

Has ap - peared to show the awe - some___ worth, of a
And they___ hope that He will be so___ pleased, With the

1 (to pg. 31, meas. 35) **2**

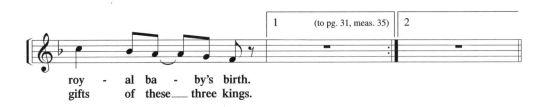

roy - al ba - by's birth.
gifts of these___ three kings.

Choir

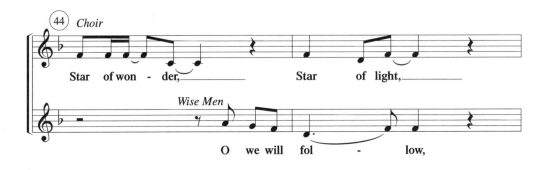

Star of won - der,___ Star of light,___

Wise Men

O we will fol - low,

Star with roy - al___ beau - ty bright.___

Yes, we will fol - low.

West - ward lead - ing still___ pro - ceed - ing,

Guide us to___ your per - fect light!

Choir

Star of won - der,_____ Star of light,_____

Wise Men

O we will fol - low,

Star with roy - al_____ beau - ty bright._____

Yes, we will fol - low.

West - ward lead - ing still___ pro - ceed - ing,

34

Guide us to___ your per - fect light!

Guide us to___your per - fect light!   Star of won - der!

VEGA: Hey, Moon, I've got a little interstellar matter I need to bounce off your lunar surface. It really burns me up that some of the earth dudes refuse to see the light of the glory of God! I mean, it's not like it's rocket science or anything.

MOON: Well, Vega, from the fourth day of Creation I've been observing the earth and reflecting on the Creator's love for the earthlings. They are His most special creation, made in His own image; to know Him and, even, to become His children; *(music starts)* something more wondrous than the stars can comprehend.

Consider my friend, the law of gravity. Gravity keeps me in my continual flight around the earth, locked in eternal orbit. Earthlings have something like gravity inside of them; a pull that keeps drawing them toward the Creator. On their journey through life they must decide whether they will move toward the Creator and His love, or reject Him. The love and the forgiveness that Jesus brought to them on that first Christmas day is always there. If they will just look to Him and accept Him as their Savior He'll light their way.

He'll Light Your Way

Words and Music by
DON and LORIE MARSH
Arranged by Don Marsh

1. Tho' you can't see a - round the cor - ner,
2. Ev - 'ry - one has a need for Son - light,

And the fu - ture is so un - clear,
Ev - 'ry heart is so dark with sin,

Close your eyes, look in - side your heart, find Him
Til the light of the Sav - ior's love shines with-

near.
in.

Take a step in the
Know the peace and the

(It would be appropriate at this time for the Pastor to lead in a prayer of Salvation or give some other opportunity for those in the congregation to make a response.)

(music starts)

QUASAR: So, Jesus, the Morning Star, came to bring the earthlings the true Light.

MOON: Yes, Quasar, Jesus said, "I am the Light of the world. Whoever follows me will never walk in darkness, but will have the light of life." *(John 8:12, NIV)* All they have to do is turn to Him, ask for forgiveness, and their lives will be filled with light.

The Light of the World Is Jesus

PHILIP P. BLISS,
DON and LORIE MARSH

PHILIP P. BLISS
Arranged by Don Marsh

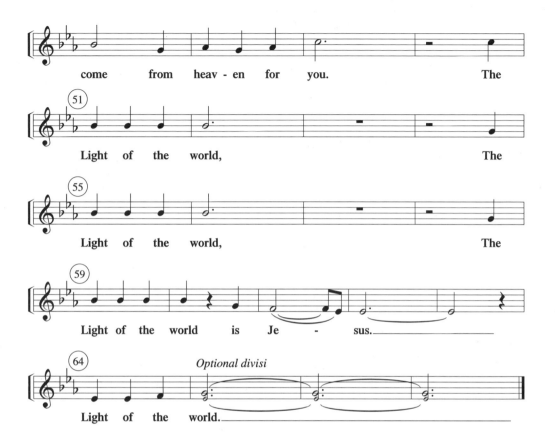

come from heav - en for you. The

Light of the world, The

Light of the world, The

Light of the world is Je - sus.

Light of the world.

Optional divisi

MOON *(building)*: Thank you for joining us here in our observatory for our star stories. As you look into the heavens this Christmas season, know that we are smiling down on you in your celebration of the birth of Jesus. We have fulfilled our mission tonight by illuminating the truth of the Christmas story and revealing the glory of God. *(music begins)*

Heaven and Nature Sing
Reprise

Words and Music by
DON and LORIE MARSH
Arranged by Don Marsh

*"Joy to the World"
Opt: add congregation

Joy to the world! the Lord is come; Let earth re-ceive her King. Let ev-'ry heart pre-pare Him room, And heav'n and na-ture sing, And heav'n and na-ture sing, And heav'n, and heav'n and na-ture sing.

heav-en and na - ture sing._____ When

heav - en,____ when heav-en and na - ture sing._____

_____ When heav - en,____ when heav-en and na - ture

sing._____ Heav-en and na - ture sing!